ROCK-OLOGY
The Hard Facts
About Rocks

Is Sand a Rock?

by Ellen Lawrence

Consultants:

Shawn W. Wallace
Department of Earth and Planetary Sciences
American Museum of Natural History, New York, New York

Kimberly Brenneman, PhD
National Institute for Early Education Research, Rutgers University
New Brunswick, New Jersey

BEARPORT
PUBLISHING

New York, New York

Credits

Cover, © Nikola Bilic/Shutterstock, and © Johnny Habell/Shutterstock; 2–3, © photka/Shutterstock; 4, © Martina_L/Shutterstock; 4–5, © Len44ik/Shutterstock; 6–7, © Sergio Stakhnyk/Shutterstock; 8, © okawa somchai; 8–9, © Dr. Gary Greenberg/Sandgrains.com; 10–11, © Shutterstock; 12, © Ragnar Th Sigurdsson/Arctic Images/Alamy; 13, © Gary Yim/Shutterstock; 14–15, © Maxim Petrichuk/Shutterstock; 15L, © Lenar Musin/Shutterstock; 15R, © James A. Harris/Shutterstock; 16–17, © Dr. Gary Greenberg/Sandgrains.com; 17, © Jolanta Wojcicka /Shutterstock, © John A. Anderson/Shutterstock, and © Pix4Pix/Shutterstock; 18T, © Niels van Kampenhout/Alamy; 18B, © Wikipedia Creative Commons; 19, © Bill Florence/Shutterstock; 20, © BlueOrange Studio/Shutterstock; 21, © Leonux/Shutterstock; 21B, © Doctor Jools/Shutterstock; 22, © kearia/Shutterstock, © Maen CG/Shutterstock, © Micha Klootwijk/Shutterstock, and © wavebreakmedia/Shutterstock; 23TL, © MatteoNannelli/Shutterstock; 23TR, © Marco Mayer/Shutterstock; 23BL, © Nastya22; 23BR, © Netfalls-Remy Musser/Shutterstock.

Publisher: Kenn Goin
Editorial Director: Adam Siegel
Creative Director: Spencer Brinker
Project Editor: Natalie Lunis
Photo Researcher: Ruby Tuesday Books Ltd

Library of Congress Cataloging-in-Publication Data

Lawrence, Ellen, 1967– author.
 Is sand a rock? / by Ellen Lawrence.
    pages cm. — (Rock-ology)
 Audience: Ages 7–12.
 Includes bibliographical references and index.
 ISBN 978-1-62724-301-8 (library binding) — ISBN 1-62724-301-1 (library binding)
 1. Sand—Juvenile literature. 2. Weathering—Juvenile literature. I. Title.
 TN939.L39 2015
 553.6'22—dc23
                          2014014022

For more information, write to Bearport Publishing Company, Inc., 45 West 21st Street, Suite 3B, New York, New York 10010. Printed in the United States of America.

10 9 8 7 6 5 4 3 2

Contents

So Many Grains of Sand

It's fun to spend the day on a sandy beach.

You can build sand castles or make pictures in wet sand.

You can push your toes into the sand's squishy softness.

Have you ever wondered, though, what sand is made of?

Also, where do all those grains of sand come from?

Every single grain of sand on Earth is different. No two grains have the same shape.

Crashing Waves

One way that sand forms is when waves crash against rocky cliffs.

Being hit by the waves makes the cliffs slowly start to crack and crumble.

Tiny pieces of rock fall into the sea.

Then the pieces are washed up on the shore.

Each one is a grain of sand.

Over time, trillions of grains of sand pile up on the shore and form a beach.

Sometimes large chunks of rock break off from cliffs and fall into the ocean. There, the rocks smash into one another and break into smaller and smaller pieces. These rocks also become sand.

rocky cliffs

waves

Sand Up Close

The sand on a beach can feel soft and powdery.

So it might be hard to believe that it comes from hard, solid rock.

When sand is viewed under a **microscope**, however, the tiny chunks of rock can be seen.

Surprisingly, they might look very different from one another.

That's because not all the grains of sand on the beach came from rocky cliffs.

Where did the rest come from?

sand

This photograph of sand was taken by a powerful microscope. The grains of sand in the picture are 125 times bigger than in real life.

Choose three grains of sand in the picture and describe them. What color is each one? What does its shape remind you of?

From Mountain to Ocean

Some of the sand on a beach might have started out on a mountainside.

When it rains, water flows down a mountain's rocky slopes.

The water wears away the rock, and tiny pieces break off.

Then the rainwater trickles into a river, and the rock goes along with it.

In time, the river carries the rock from the mountain into the ocean.

Then the rock is washed up on a beach as sand.

Many large lakes have sandy beaches. The sand comes from mountains and other rocky places that may be many miles away. The sand is carried to the lakes' shores by rivers.

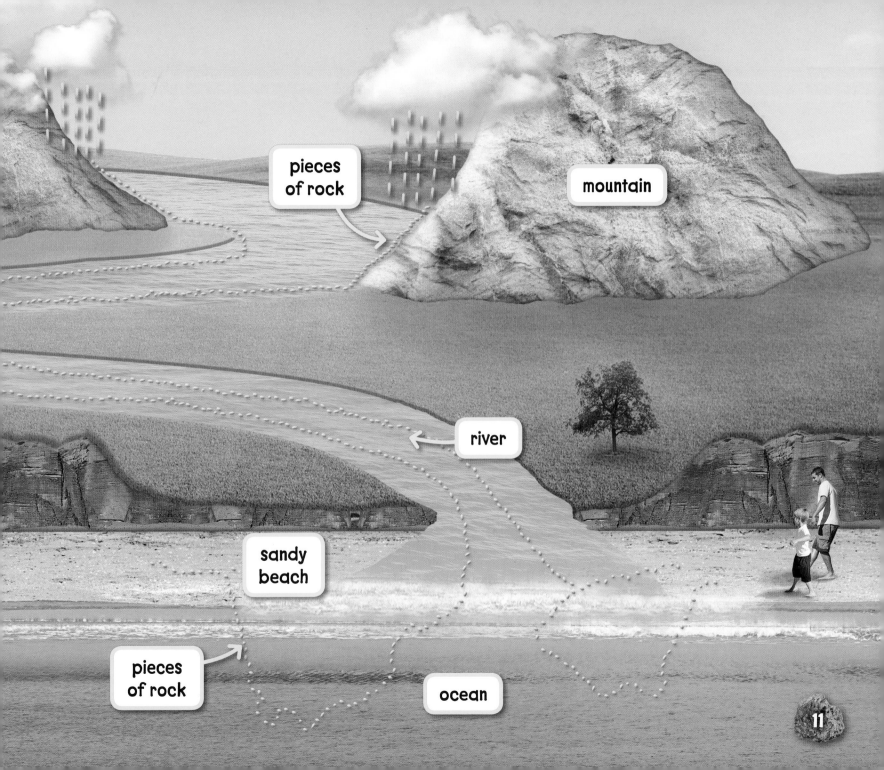

pieces
of rock

mountain

river

sandy
beach

pieces
of rock

ocean

11

Freezing and Cracking

There is another way that the weather can help make sand.

Sometimes, melted snow trickles into a crack in a rock.

When the weather gets colder, the water freezes.

As the water turns to ice, it expands, or gets bigger, and pushes the crack open.

As the rock cracks and splits, tiny pieces of it break off.

Then melted snow or rain washes these grains of sand into rivers and out to sea.

Scientists can study sand on a beach to find out what kind of rock it is made up of. Once they know, they can figure out which mountain or rocky place the sand came from.

crack

① There is a crack in a rock.

② Water gets into the crack and freezes. The ice expands.

③ The rock splits open.

Sometimes sand from a desert may travel many miles to a beach. How do you think this sand is moved?

pieces of broken rock

Traveling the World

Sand can be moved from place to place by the wind.

Sometimes the wind blows across a sandy **desert** and picks up grains of sand.

Then it can carry them long distances to a beach.

Sand from the Sahara Desert in Africa has been blown to beaches in Florida.

That's a journey of more than 5,000 miles (8,000 km)!

sand blowing across a desert

Just like rain, wind can wear away rocks and make sand. How? When wind blows, it often picks up loose pieces of sand or dirt. The flying sand or dirt then rubs against large rocks. As a result, tiny pieces—which are new grains of sand— break off.

Sahara Desert

Miami Beach, Florida

Sand from Shells

On many beaches, most of the sand is made up of pieces of rock.

Some sand, however, is made from the **shells** of animals such as crabs and clams.

When these creatures die, their shells get crushed and broken in the ocean.

Then the tiny pieces of shell get washed up on beaches.

Like shells, the skeletons of ocean animals such as corals, sea urchins, and sponges also break into tiny pieces. Then they get washed up on beaches as sand, too.

a piece of a sponge's skeleton

a piece of coral

a piece of shell

Green Sand, Black Sand

Sand can be white, gray, yellow, brown, pink, red, green, and even black!

That's because sand gets its color from **minerals**—the hard substances that make up rocks.

Minerals can be many different colors.

In Hawaii, there is a beach with greenish-brown sand.

The sand comes from a rock that contains a green-colored mineral called olivine.

a beach with greenish-brown sand

grains of olivine viewed under a microscope

Hawaii also has beaches with black sand. This sand is made from a kind of rock called basalt.

19

Tiny but Amazing

Next time you are at the beach, take a close-up look at the sand.

Perhaps it is made from the shells of tiny sea animals.

Maybe the tiny sand grains started out as part of a rocky cliff or mountain.

Also, think about this.

You might be standing on sand that was once part of a faraway desert!

Some beaches have pale pink sand. The sand gets its color from billions of tiny pieces of broken pink shells.

a close-up view of pink sand from a beach

Science Lab

Make Some Sand

You can try making sand using small rocks, or stones, from a garden or beach.

You will need:

- 10 stones (try to find different kinds)
- Metal container with a tight lid, such as a coffee can
- Water
- Coffee filter

I. Place the stones in the container and pour in enough water to cover them. Put the lid on the container. Make sure it's on tight.

2. Now shake the container 1,000 times! Try splitting the shakes into 10 groups of 100. You don't have to do all of them at the same time, or even on the same day.

3. When you have shaken the container 1,000 times, remove the stones from the water.

4. Ask a helper to hold a coffee filter over a sink. Slowly pour the water into the filter.

Describe what you see in the filter.

How is what happens inside the can like what happens in real life?

(See page 24 for the answers.)

Science Words

desert (DEZ-urt) dry land with few plants and little rainfall; deserts are often covered in sand

microscope (MYE-kruh-skohp) a tool or machine used to see things that are too small to see with the eyes alone

minerals (MIN-ur-uhlz) the solid substances found in nature that make up rocks

shells (SHELZ) hard outer coverings that protect the bodies of some animals, such as clams, mussels, and crabs

Index

Read More

Mattern, Joanne. *Sand, Silt, and Mud and the Rock Cycle.* New York: PowerKids Press (2006).

Owen, Ruth. *Science and Craft Projects with Rocks and Soil (Get Crafty Outdoors).* New York: PowerKids Press (2013).

Prager, Ellen J. *Sand.* Washington, D.C.: National Geographic (2000).

Learn More Online

To learn more about rocks and sand, visit
www.bearportpublishing.com/Rock-ology

About the Author

Ellen Lawrence lives in the United Kingdom. Her favorite books to write are those about nature and animals. In fact, the first book Ellen bought for herself, when she was six years old, was the story of a gorilla named Patty Cake that was born in New York's Central Park Zoo.

Answers

Page 22: In the filter, you will find tiny grains of rock. Together, the grains make sand. When the rocks are shaken, it is like what happens to small pieces of rock in a river. The rocks are smashed against one another by the rushing river water. As a result, they break into tiny pieces, or grains.